"This clear and concise introduction to key concepts in Stoicism is thoughtful and engaging. It uses texts mostly from Epictetus as each chapter's starting point, and insightful discussions of well-chosen examples illustrate how Stoics discern the nuances of various practical situations to find a path to a worthwhile life. The authors succeed in making Stoic thinking appeal to a wide audience."

— **William O. Stephens**, professor emeritus of philosophy at Creighton University and author of *Marcus Aurelius: A Guide for the Perplexed* and *Stoic Ethics: Epictetus and Happiness as Freedom*

WHAT IS
STOICISM?

WHAT IS STOICISM?

A BRIEF
AND ACCESSIBLE
OVERVIEW

TANNER CAMPBELL
& KAI WHITING

New World Library
Novato, California

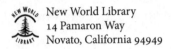

New World Library
14 Pamaron Way
Novato, California 94949

Text design by Megan Colman

Library of Congress Cataloging-in-Publication Data

Names: Campbell, Tanner, author. | Whiting, Kai, author.
Title: What is stoicism? : a brief and accessible overview / Tanner Campbell & Kai Whiting.
Description: Novato, California : New World Library, [2024] | Includes bibliographical references. | Summary: "An easy, jargon-free introduction to Stoic philosophy and its relevance to modern life. Topics include: the three pillars of Stoic philosophy (logic, physics, and ethics), the Stoic ideal of living in accordance with nature, and the question of whether belief in God is necessary for practicing Stoicism"-- Provided by publisher.
Identifiers: LCCN 2024023026 (print) | LCCN 2024023027 (ebook) | ISBN 9781608689446 (paperback) | ISBN 9781608689453 (epub)
Subjects: LCSH: Stoics. | Conduct of life.
Classification: LCC B528 .C27 2024 (print) | LCC B528 (ebook) | DDC 188--dc23/eng/20240702
LC record available at https://lccn.loc.gov/2024023026
LC ebook record available at https://lccn.loc.gov/2024023027

First printing, November 2024
ISBN 978-1-60868-944-6
Ebook ISBN 978-1-60868-945-3
Printed in Canada

10   9   8   7   6   5   4   3   2   1

New World Library is committed to protecting our natural environment. This book is made of material from well-managed FSC®-certified forests and other controlled sources.

To Ross and Cailean, the strongest arguments for there being more than one Good. I love you.

— Tanner

To Taru and LGC, only you will truly know if I am ever worthy of being called a Stoic.

— Kai

CONTENTS

PROLOGUE

IN WRITING THIS BOOK, we opened ourselves up to the challenge of creating a brief, accessible, and accurate overview of Stoicism in as few words, and as plainly, as possible. We wanted to do this because, while there are plenty of books about Stoicism, many (not all) of them are either too academic or too shallow. We thought something short, which could be read in a single afternoon, would be useful to those wondering what Stoicism is and whether it is the right life philosophy for them. We also wanted to help those already casually acquainted with Stoicism to delve deeper into the philosophy and expand their understanding of it. Regardless of why you are reading this book, we hope it does more than explain Stoicism. We hope that it inspires you to adopt Stoicism as a life philosophy and that, subsequently, you are encouraged to think more frequently and deeply about your roles and responsibilities so you can better play your part in improving the world.

If, however, you decide that Stoicism isn't the

right life philosophy for you, that's absolutely fine! If this is the conclusion you arrive at after reading our book, we will be only too happy that you'll have reached such a decision through a more coherent and accurate understanding of what Stoic philosophy is. We may consider Stoicism to be a cure-all for many of humanity's ills, but that doesn't mean we're right or that you must feel the same way.

Regardless of the conclusions you come to concerning Stoicism, we'd like to thank you for reading our book and for participating in this whistle-stop tour of Stoic philosophy.

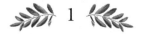

WHAT IS STOICISM?

I made a prosperous voyage when I suffered a shipwreck.

— ZENO OF CITIUM, founder of Stoicism, as relayed by DIOGENES LAERTIUS, *Lives of the Eminent Philosophers*, 7.1.4

STOICISM IS AN ANCIENT Greek/Roman philosophy built largely upon a virtue ethics framework. It was founded by Zeno of Citium in 300 BCE. Prior to founding Stoicism, Zeno was a merchant selling a dye known as "Royal Purple." This dye was so expensive that it was used exclusively by the wealthy elite to stain their clothing, primarily as a way of signaling their wealth and status.

While Zeno was en route to deliver a batch of this dye to the Athenian market, the ship that he was traveling on was caught in a storm. All cargo was lost to the sea, but Zeno survived. This turn of events left him a penniless immigrant, homeless on the streets of Athens with no obvious financial prospects.

Faced with the challenge of enduring this new reality, and unsure of what to do next, Zeno journeyed more than one hundred miles, on foot, to visit the Oracle of Delphi — a woman renowned for her prophecies and wisdom. The Oracle advised Zeno to "take on the pallor of the dead." After some reflection, he interpreted her advice to mean that he should "study the wisdom of the ancients."

Upon his return to Athens, Zeno stopped at a small bookshop and, so the story goes, began reading Xenophon's *Memorabilia* (a work that is mostly a defense of the Greek philosopher Socrates). As Zeno read, he was struck by the greatness of those mentioned in *Memorabilia* and, turning to the shopkeeper, asked, "Where can I find men like these?" It just so happened that another famous philosopher, Crates the Cynic, was passing by at that very moment. "Follow that man," replied the bookshop owner, pointing at Crates. Zeno did as he was told. Crates the Cynic became the first of many mentors to provide Zeno with the pieces of a puzzle that would eventually lead to his founding of Stoic philosophy.

It was important to Zeno that his philosophy be accessible to all. He decided that the best way to go about it was to teach from beneath the cover of the *Stoa Poikile* (meaning "Painted Porch"). This porch is what gave Stoicism its name. The

Stoa Poikile was a public walkway and portico connected to a marketplace where all — the rich and the poor, the free and the enslaved — went about their daily business. Therefore, all of them could, as they walked past, listen to Zeno's radical message: anyone who is capable of reason, and who has a genuine desire to strive for a good character, can flourish. By this Zeno meant that they could aspire to *live a life worthy of being lived* (in other words, they could achieve *eudaimonia*); that no matter their gender, financial status, place of birth, or family standing, they could become good people.

What does it mean, to "become good"?

The ancient Stoics had a unique understanding of the word and concept of "good." Contemporary peoples tend to understand and conceptualize "good" (and goodness) very differently from the ancient Stoics. Consequently, this brings us to the first of many important nuances that newcomers to Stoicism tend to overlook. And so, the ancient Stoic understanding of "good" provides us with the perfect starting point in our exploration of what Stoicism actually is.

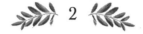

2

Good and Bad

For in every area of study, we're seeking to learn how a good and virtuous person may discover the path that he should follow in life and the way in which he should conduct himself.

— Epictetus, *Discourses* 1.7.2

People today use the word *good* in several different ways. For example, we could have a "good" day, meaning a pleasurable one, or, alternatively, we could tell someone we feel "good" when what we mean is we feel *okay*. A car can be "good," and we can tell our dog that he is a "good boy," but do we mean the same thing in all these cases? Clearly, we do not. We might consider a car to be "good" because it successfully gets us from point A to point B without any issues, while we may refer to our dog as "good" because our pet cheers us up when we're feeling low or helps us feel needed and loved.

Words can, and often do, change in meaning over time. In the nineteenth century, for example, the word *cool* nearly always meant "cold." In the twenty-first century, however, *cool* almost always means something like "all right," "great," or "interesting." Likewise, the word *good*, when used in a purely Stoic context, means something different than when it is used in a non-Stoic context.

In Stoicism, the word *good* refers to only one thing: Virtue. For the Stoics, Virtue is the *only* good. To be virtuous — to possess Virtue — is to have cultivated a perfect moral character, one that is just, temperate, wise, and courageous (more on this in chapter 7).

To be clear, in Stoicism, Virtue isn't *a* good; it isn't the *greatest* good; it is the *only* good. This means that even something as seemingly positive as world peace isn't "good" in the Stoic sense of the word.

In Stoicism, there is also only one bad: Vice. To be vicious is to have an immoral character, one that is unjust, cowardly, ignorant, and lacking in self-control (e.g., greedy or prone to rage).

Again, to be clear, in Stoicism, Vice isn't a *sort* of bad; it isn't the *worst kind* of bad; it is the *only* bad. This means that even something like slavery isn't "bad" in the Stoic sense of the word.

Now, having just read the previous sentence,

you may be tempted to abandon all interest in Stoicism entirely — but hold on a moment! We promise your aversion is misplaced.

Remember, the Stoic understanding of *good* and *bad* is not the same as our contemporary understanding of these words. When the Stoics say, "Virtue is the only good," they aren't saying that world peace doesn't matter or that it is unworthy of pursuing. Instead, they are highlighting that world peace, in and of itself, isn't always something positive.

Imagine, for example, if we defined *world peace* as "the absence of war." The absence of war could, arguably, be achieved by installing a global dictator who, through coercion and fear, created a world that didn't know war. In this case, the Stoics would argue that it could well be within our responsibility to bring war against that dictator — thus destroying "world peace" — as this is what the virtuous person would, and therefore must, do in such a situation.

Likewise, when the Stoics say, "Vice is the only bad," they aren't saying, for example, that slavery doesn't matter or that we shouldn't work toward abolishing it. However, it may well be that acquiring slaves is the right thing to do under certain circumstances (albeit very few). One such example would be the choice to participate in the legal process of manumission. *Manumission* is the acquiring of slaves for the express purpose of freeing them. Manumission was practiced in ancient Greece and Rome and is *still practiced today*. Surely no good person would refuse to purchase a slave in order to free that slave from bondage simply because they felt uncomfortable about being a so-called slave master during the time it takes them to sign the release papers to free said slave.

This sort of reasoning is why Stoics do not declare moral absolutes. *Context matters*, and no one rule (or set of rules) can ensure that the right thing is done in every circumstance. That said, turning a blind eye to slavery, or working against world peace, would very likely, at least in most contexts, say something terrible about our character. And if the Stoics are adamant about anything, they are adamant that possessing a terrible (vicious) character is bad.

Stoicism is a virtue-centric philosophy, and Stoics believe that the purpose of a human's life is to achieve a state of eudaimonia (a life worthy of being lived). The *only* way a person can do this is by developing a good (virtuous) character. The person who possesses such a character never acts badly (immorally). In fact, they are said to be incapable of doing so. If everyone were to achieve a virtuous character, there would be world peace. There would be no slavery.

To the Stoics, there is nothing better, nor more important, than Virtue and the development of a virtuous character (and nothing more terrible than Vice, that is, the possession of a vicious character).

In Stoicism, everything that isn't either Virtue (good) or Vice (bad/evil) is an "indifferent" (this includes world peace, slavery, and everything in between these two extreme examples).

The Stoic understanding of the word *indifferent* is what we explore next, because it also does not mean what you may think it does. As we navigate the forthcoming chapter, it is important to keep the following in your mind: while Stoics identify Virtue as the only good, and Vice as the only bad, this does not mean that they think these two things are the only things that matter.

3

VIRTUE AND INDIFFERENTS

Some things are good, others bad, and others again indifferent; that the virtues and what partakes in the virtues are good, while things of the opposite nature are bad; and that wealth, health, and reputation are indifferent.

— EPICTETUS, *Discourses* 2.19.15

WE HAVE USED THE WORD *Virtue* no fewer than a dozen times across all the pages leading up to this sentence, but we have yet to define exactly what it is. So, what *is* Virtue? Virtue is a special kind of knowledge: the knowledge of how to *live excellently*. When someone possesses Virtue, they know how to perfectly conduct themselves in all circumstances (in chapters 7 and 8, we explain how one goes about attaining this knowledge).

Because it is a kind of knowledge, Virtue is expressed through an individual's choices (since we make choices based on what we know, or believe, to be right/true). Our choices, then, say something about the *quality of our character*. An example you may recognize: imagine if the CEO of a company, who has traditionally paid holiday bonuses to their employees at the end of the year, decided, in an attempt to increase corporate profits, to replace all employee bonuses with annual memberships to the "Jelly of the Month Club."[1] That would say something rather disconcerting about that CEO's character!

Now that you have a baseline understanding of what Virtue is, we can move on to indifferents.

In Stoicism, the word *indifferent* (and specifically its plural form, *indifferents*) is often confused with the English term and concept of "indifference." The latter is used to refer to something we don't care about, something we find trivial or otherwise unimportant or irrelevant. However, the Stoic use of the word *indifferent* refers to something that has *no impact whatsoever* on a person's ability to develop a virtuous character (or, alternatively, to possess a vicious character).

To better understand the Stoic concept of "indifferents," let's return to our examples in the previous chapter: world peace and slavery. World peace is an indifferent because its existence has no impact upon whether individuals possess virtuous characters (or are capable of working toward possessing them). We can easily see the truth of this by imagining all the people who have chosen to behave badly during times when the world was at peace! Likewise, being a slave cannot prevent a person from developing a virtuous character (nor can it protect them from cultivating a vicious one).

There is even such an example in Stoicism's history.

Epictetus, a Stoic teacher and philosopher, whose quote we began this chapter with, was born a slave. His mother was a slave as well, and (as Scott Aikin and William O. Stephens point out) Epictetus's name actually means "acquired."[2] In spite of this, Epictetus still went on to establish his own philosophical school and dedicate much of his life to helping others work toward the betterment of their character, through the attainment of Virtue.

By contrast, one of Epictetus's "masters," who had also been a slave, is reported to have cruelly broken Epictetus's leg while disciplining him.

Both men were slaves, but only one of them was actively working toward Virtue. It was not their enslavement that directed their behavior or dictated the quality of their moral character; it was their individual choices. Our choices are *not* indifferents — our choices, as we mentioned earlier, reflect the quality of our character.

But wouldn't world peace make it a little bit easier for people to develop virtuous characters?

No. The challenges facing a person who is free from war are still numerous. For example, one can still give in to greed, or murder someone, regardless of how peaceful a state the world is or isn't presently in. Becoming a good (virtuous) person isn't aided (or hindered) by external circumstances or events.

Since a virtuous character is an internally developed characteristic, nothing can make developing it more or less difficult except a person's natural disposition as an individual. That said, a person can be more or less receptive to the sculpting of their character toward Virtue — some people are like granite, while others are like clay.

It could also be argued that there is a *greater impetus* for developing a virtuous character among individuals facing extreme external adversities compared to those facing none or very few. After all, what would prompt us to consider the quality of our character if we had all the money in the world and very little self-awareness, and we could all too easily use our wealth to rectify the consequences of our vicious behavior (e.g., bribe a law official in order to avoid jail time)?

It should come as no surprise, then, that Epictetus, one of the most well-regarded ancient Stoics, was himself, as already stated, a slave prior to becoming a Stoic philosopher. Perhaps it is also no surprise that the founder of Stoicism, Zeno of Citium (whom we have already met) sketched the path to a flourishing life only after suffering a shipwreck and becoming a homeless, penniless merchant with nothing to sell.

Indifferents: Preferred vs. Dispreferred

A *preferred indifferent* is something we rationally deem to be beneficial to pursue or possess. Life, for example, is, all things being equal, preferable to death because it naturally promotes wellness. For the Stoics, life remains preferred over death as long as its pursuit doesn't reflect negatively upon our moral character by requiring us to behave viciously. On the other hand, a *dispreferred indifferent* is something we rationally deem to be detrimental for us to pursue or possess. Therefore, it is something we would do well to avoid, unless its avoidance negatively affects our moral character.[3] There is a third "subcategory" of indifferents: inconsequential indifferent. However, given their inconsequential nature, we've decided not to discuss them here.

To illustrate, world peace is *typically* preferred over its absence, making it (more often than not) what Stoics would refer to as a "preferred indifferent." However, world peace is not *always* preferred, as we explained with the example of a global tyrant ruling over a world without war. World peace under a tyrant is then what the Stoics refer to as a "dispreferred indifferent" and war, at least in this case, would become a "preferred indifferent."

Money, as another example, is an indifferent in that the amount we have, whether a little or a lot, has no impact on our character either. Rather, it is how we *use* or *regard* our money that says something about who we are. Certainly, our physical well-being (up to a point) improves if we have at least some money. It therefore isn't "un-Stoic" to prefer wealth over poverty, so long as that preference doesn't interfere with the cultivation of a good character. This means that if we suddenly find out that the *way* we make money has become a poor reflection of our character, then we are obliged to do something about it!

Imagine the husband who accepts a promotion at work to improve his social standing, but to the detriment of his family's well-being (perhaps he must work so many hours that he cannot be present for his children and spouse). There is nothing wrong, from the Stoic perspective, with this father making more money, but there *is* something wrong with him making more money at all costs.

There is also something wrong with him choosing not to rectify the situation upon realizing the error of his ways.

Many contemporary Stoics incorrectly assume that money is *always* a preferred indifferent, because who would prefer to be dirt poor over being filthy rich? However, to think this way is to entirely misunderstand the concept of Stoic indifferents. If something were always preferred it would always be good — but the only thing that is always good is Virtue, because how could the knowledge of how to live excellently ever be anything but good?

Money, like world peace, can become dispreferred. Imagine a gambling addict who is working to overcome their addiction. If such a person found themselves in Las Vegas struggling with temptation, would it be preferable for them to have access to money at that precise moment? What are they most likely to do with that money? Almost certainly something that reflects the viciousness (absence of Virtue) of their character. In such a case it would be preferable for them to have no money at all.

What about a dispreferred indifferent such as cancer? How could cancer ever be preferred? Well, it depends on the alternative. If the alternative is immediate death, it may be that we would prefer to have cancer along with the opportunity to fight it and survive. Consider this example further, and regardless of whether we survive the disease: Perhaps cancer, and coming face-to-face with our own mortality, finally encourages us to reflect on our difficult relationship with our parents. If we decided, while gravely ill, to take action to mend our broken relationship, how would this affect our character? Almost certainly in a positive way. So, in this case, our cancer diagnosis provides the opportunity for us to choose to move toward Virtue, not away from it. Stoically speaking, it is *always* better to be ill and moving toward Virtue than to be vicious and healthy.

The Stoics believe a person should work on distinguishing whether an indifferent is preferred or dispreferred on a case-by-case basis. There is no sweeping rule that states "X is always preferred" or "Y is always dispreferred." On the contrary, our decisions to pursue (or avoid) the various indifferents in our lives are arrived at through thoughtful consideration of the *context* surrounding the making of such decisions. Stoics aim to do this in every single situation, so context is paramount when it comes to making the right (morally appropriate) or wrong (morally inappropriate) decisions in life.

It is important to note that simply knowing what an indifferent is, and knowing that indifferents have no impact on our moral character, isn't enough to prevent us from *reacting* to indifferents in ways that do impact our moral character.

Imagine someone calls us ugly, fat, or stupid. These words are not capable of impacting our Virtue. However, this doesn't change the fact that someone calling us a horrible name may well result in our *choosing* to act viciously in response. We might, for instance, get so angry that we punch our insulter in the face. What would this action say about our character? Did we have no choice but to react in this way? The Stoics would say that such behavior reflects the absence of Virtue and that, outside of extreme circumstances, we always have a choice as to how we think and act. An example of an extreme case would be experiencing a medically induced or drug-induced mental state that severely impairs our cognitive ability, or experiencing a psychotic episode. So, then, how Stoics approach thinking, choosing, and acting is what we discuss next.

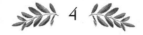

4

Impressions and Assent

The most important task of a philosopher, and his first task, is to test out impressions and distinguish between them, and not to accept any impression unless it has been duly tested.

— Epictetus, *Discourses* 1.20.7

If a friend is an hour late meeting us for dinner, we might generate some theories as to why that might be. If they have been late on several occasions, we might think something like "He doesn't care about our plans. I bet he hasn't even left home yet. What a flake!"

The story we have created in our head, in response to our friend's tardiness, is an "impression." An impression is what we *believe* is happening (or what we believe to be true). At this stage, we don't know for certain why our friend is late, but we have assumed they're late because they don't care to be on time.

If we decide that our "theory" is correct and we proceed to believe it as fact, the Stoics say that we have "assented to an impression." However, an impression should be assented to only when we have sufficient information to justify it. Let's say our friend texted us, "Oh man, I totally forgot! I haven't even left yet!" We would be correct to assent to our impression that, for today at least, we aren't on our friend's list of priorities. Without this information, though, the Stoics would instruct us to hold off from assenting, as doing so would risk the belief of a falsehood. For the Stoics, falsely assenting is problematic because if we believe too many falsehoods our overall perception of the world becomes warped, and it suddenly becomes much harder to reason ourselves toward decisions that move us closer to Virtue and away from Vice. After all, how can we correctly select right from wrong (in any given situation) if we have totally misunderstood reality?

Returning to the example of someone calling us an unkind name: We might, before choosing to assent to the impression that being called an unkind name hurts us in some way, ask ourselves whether the name we were called is an accurate reflection of reality. If the answer is no, why assent to the impression that the words refer to us in any meaningful way? Why come to any conclusion other than that such a silly comment has no power over us? It might have been said as an insult, but that doesn't mean that we must take it as one. It is *up to us to choose* how we react to the words of others. The fact that another person has tried to offend us says something negative about *their* character. How we respond says something about *ours*.

However, should our perception change if we believe there to be some truth to an insult? What if someone calls us fat and we *are* at an unhealthy weight (clinically obese) because of our poor lifestyle choices? Perhaps we have had it in our mind for some time that we want to become healthier, and the insult triggers us because we know it is an accurate reflection of reality. Perhaps we assent to the impression that we are, in fact, at an unhealthy weight, and we do, in fact, feel that something needs to be done about it. Maybe we assent to another impression: that our choice *not* to address our health concerns says something negative about our character.

It might appear that we are contradicting ourselves here. On the one hand, we've assured you that something like a person's weight, in and of itself, says nothing about their character. But now it might seem that we're saying the opposite. If you're picking up on this, that's great because it means you're reading critically, trying to suss out the truth of what's being said (how Stoic of you!) — but let us not gloss over your concern, because there is nuance we want you to comprehend.

Being called fat cannot be bad (vicious) because being called a name doesn't damage our character. Being at an unhealthy weight, on the other hand, *might* (not definitely, but might) speak ill of our character if we have, through our choices, created our unhealthy body even when it was in our power to do otherwise. In short, if we choose to eat unhealthy food, not exercise, and treat our body poorly, then we have made some inappropriate choices. If, on the other hand, we choose to eat well, but are overweight because of a hormonal imbalance, then our extra layers of fat say nothing as to the quality of our character because it was not our choices that led to the present state of our health.

In other words, not caring about the health and fitness of our body does suggest something negative about our character. However, it could be that we care very deeply about our body's health and fitness yet can do next to nothing about it. Let's say we find ourselves wrongly convicted of a crime and, thus, imprisoned. In this scenario, we may have no control over our diet and be very restricted in our ability to exercise. However, if we are intent on reducing the impact our imprisonment is having on our health, and we choose to exercise whenever we are able to do so, then we are doing everything we can to cultivate a virtuous character despite our externally imposed restrictions. This is a key Stoic lesson: Our Virtue is a product of our choices, thoughts, and actions. It does not hinge on outcomes or external conditions. In the above example, we are unhealthy, but not through any fault of our own. From the Stoic point of view, health is an indifferent, as we cannot choose the state of our health. It is typically a preferred indifferent, but we do not need to possess it in order to live a life worthy of being lived. That said, the choice to not do what we are able to do for the sake of our health *is* vicious. This means any state of health can be appropriate so long as reasonable efforts toward becoming healthier are being made (or an insurmountable outside force is preventing any such efforts).

With all this talk of choice and control, we now turn to another Stoic concept: the "Dichotomy of Control."

THE DICHOTOMY
OF CONTROL

Some things are within our power, while others are not. Within our power are opinion, motivation, desire, aversion, and, in a word, whatever is of our own doing; not within our power are our body, our property, reputation, office, and, in a word, whatever is not of our own doing.

— EPICTETUS, *The Encheiridion* 1.1

EPICTETUS IS ONE OF THE THREE most well-known Stoics (the other two are Marcus Aurelius and Seneca the Younger). He is also the one who came up with an idea known, in Greek, as *Eph' ēmin*, or "that which is up to us," a concept contemporarily referred to as the "Dichotomy of Control." Michael Tremblay conceptualizes the "control" aspect as being more like "the ability to decide."[1]

Regardless of the exact terminology used,

however, the Dichotomy of Control is a way of framing the universal truth that some things are within our power to choose, and other things are not. For example, we cannot choose the weather, but we can choose how we *feel* about it. Epictetus tells us that we exert "control" over only three things:

- our thoughts (including some of our emotions)
- our actions
- our attitudes

The fact that we can control only three things doesn't imply that we should only care about these three things. On the contrary, the Stoics view humans as *prosocial* creatures, which means we are called to care about a great many things over which we have no control. How we care about things also speaks directly to the quality of our character. An example: we cannot control our parents, but most of us would agree that, in most cases, we wouldn't be a particularly good son or daughter if we didn't care about them (for what does *not* caring about others, let alone our parents, say about our character?).

Put simply, the Dichotomy of Control isn't about learning not to care about the things (or people) we have no control over. Rather, it is about learning to accept the limits of any control we have and to consider whether certain thoughts, attitudes, or actions are appropriate (or not) given these very real limits.

Another example: We have a romantic picnic planned with our partner, and we've worked very hard to prepare for it. On the day of our date, however, we wake to find a weather forecast of severe thunderstorms. We immediately feel upset. We start to believe that everything is ruined and that the universe is plotting against us!

The Stoics teach us to examine our feelings in such moments and to ask ourselves whether being upset would somehow bring out the sun. How useful is it to be upset about any situation that cannot be remedied by our *being* upset?

In any case, being upset often throws us into a funk that might take us hours to think ourselves out of. In this state we tend not to behave well; we are more likely to act in ways that demonstrate that we are moving further from Virtue rather than nearer to it. In other words, we are more likely to forget what is and isn't in our control, to the detriment of our character. Returning to our romantic example, while our picnic plan has been ruined by the storm, our date doesn't have to be — we could always find delight in having lunch together in the living room, under a blanket fort, instead. Get stuck in a funk, though, and we might jeopardize our date altogether by choosing to sulk over that which we cannot control.

That said, if we find ourselves in a funk (or in any other kind of emotional downward spiral), the Stoics do not advocate for suppressing or ignoring our feelings. Learning to express emotions healthily is paramount to flourishing, and we cannot become more skilled at expressing (or controlling) our emotions by denying that they exist. Rather than suppressing our emotions, the Stoics advocate for better management of them through constructive self-examination, both alone and, where appropriate, with the support of others, including mentors (see Marcus Aurelius's Book 1 of *Meditations* for numerous examples). The Stoics also teach us that by realizing the limits of our control, we can limit the degree to which we allow indifferent things to negatively impact our character, which is helpful to remember the next time we find ourselves in a funk.

This is, of course, much easier said than done. The Stoics recognized this reality, which is why they used the term *prokoptôn* (plural, prokoptôntes) to highlight that the path to eudaimonia consists predominantly of both learning and character training and development. With each appropriate action, or thought, we are progressing in the right direction along that path, because we are setting about obtaining the knowledge that enables us to live excellently. So, now, let's learn more about the Stoic in training: the prokoptôn.

6

THE *PROKOPTÔN* AND *PROSOCHĒ*

Come now, show me what progress you're making in this regard. Suppose I were talking with an athlete and said, "Show me your shoulders," and he were to reply, "Look at my jumping-weights." That's quite enough of you and your weights! What I want to see is what you've achieved by use of those jumping-weights.

— EPICTETUS, *Discourses* 1.4.13

THE WORD *PROKOPTÔN* refers to a person making progress. It isn't strictly a Stoicism-related word, but in Stoicism that progress is along the Stoic path toward eudaimonia. At the end of the Stoic path is sagehood, which represents the Stoic ideal of excellence in human individuals. For now, we'll focus on how those who are prokoptôntes walk the Stoic path well — which requires us to introduce another word: *prosochē*.

Prosochē is the practice and art of paying attention. To progress along the Stoic path, we must learn to pay attention to the three things under our control: our thoughts, actions, and attitudes. We must also consistently check in with our impressions (judgments), assents, and desires. As contemporary Stoic Chris Fisher reminds us, when we reflect on Epictetus's words (in *Discourses* 4.12.19), "the practicable goal of Stoicism is not perfection; instead, it is 'to strive continuously not to commit faults,' with the realistic hope that by 'never relaxing our attention, we shall escape at least a few *faults.*'"[1]

We can consider prosochē as a state of focus during which we are being vigilant over our own actions and we are highly aware of what we are thinking and doing and of the corresponding attitude we have toward our self, toward others, and toward the situations we find ourselves in. Pierre Hadot likens prosochē to moral consciousness, where we seek to purify and rectify our intentions and motives.[2] In this regard, some might prefer to frame prosochē as a Stoic spiritual exercise of mindfulness.

How might we apply prosochē, the act of paying attention, to our day-to-day life? Epictetus gave us some clues when he instructed his students to distinguish between what was up to them and what wasn't (in *Discourses* 3.3.14–16, as translated by Robin Hard and Christopher Gill):

> One should train oneself. As soon as you leave the house at break of day, examine everyone whom you see, everyone whom you hear, and answer as if under questioning. What did you see? A handsome man or beautiful woman? Apply the rule. Does this lie within the sphere of choice, or outside it? Outside. Throw it away. What did you see? Someone grieving over the death of his child? Apply the rule. Death is something that lies outside the sphere of choice. Away with it. You met a consul? Apply the rule. What kind of thing is a consulship? One that lies outside the sphere of choice, or inside? Outside. Throw that away too, it doesn't stand the test. Away with it; it is nothing to you. If we acted in such a way and practised this exercise from morning until night, we would then have achieved something.

What can, and should, we pay attention to exactly? *The present moment.* Marcus Aurelius reminded himself of this when he wrote (in *Meditations* 3.10) that there's nothing else to pay attention to:

"Cast everything else aside, then, and hold to these few truths alone; and remember, furthermore, that each of us lives only in the present, this fleeting moment of time, and that the rest of one's life has either already been lived or lies in an unknowable future."

So, to summarize, prokoptôntes are Stoics in training or in progress, while prosochē is the practice of paying proper attention to our thoughts, attitudes, and actions. As prokoptôntes, this practice helps us move closer toward Virtue.

7

THE CARDINAL VIRTUES

Virtue is not just theoretical knowledge; it is also practical like both medical and musical knowledge.

— MUSONIUS RUFUS, *Discourses*, Lecture 6.1

IN STOICISM, THERE ARE what are called the four Cardinal Virtues:

1. Temperance
2. Justice
3. Courage
4. Wisdom

Nested within these Cardinal Virtues are "subordinate virtues" (you can call them "mini virtues" if you like), such as generosity, kindness, and honesty (and many others). For the sake of brevity, we won't go into subordinate virtues.

TEMPERANCE speaks to the ability to control oneself, to not overindulge, to not rush to assent to impressions, and so on. You can think of it as having a disposition for moderation and self-control.

JUSTICE speaks to the appropriate and fair treatment of others, including the distribution of resources (such as clean drinking water, food, or shelter). It doesn't apply only in the legal sense (like in the courts and such); it applies to *every* interaction we have with our fellow human beings and, in our view, with animals and with the rest of the planet.

COURAGE speaks to our willingness to face and endure difficult circumstances with the common good in mind. You can also think of it as doing the right thing even when doing the wrong thing is easier (or, especially, when doing the right thing will "hurt").

WISDOM allows us to navigate our lives virtuously. It involves knowing what is good or bad and how to appropriately pursue preferred indifferents and avoid dispreferred ones.

The four Cardinal Virtues are defined in such a way that they might appear to be actions — but that's not entirely accurate. Virtues aren't actions; they are character traits. The Stoic sage's character, through their choices (and therefore also their actions), *demonstrates* that they possess the four Cardinal Virtues — that they *are*, and are not merely being, courageous, just, self-controlled, and wise. To comprehend these Virtues more easily as character traits, rather than as actions, consider the following analogy: A bodybuilder can lift heavy weights correctly because they have developed muscle over time due to their persistent and well-designed training regimen. In this sense, Virtue is their ability (as encapsulated in the knowledge necessary) to properly lift the weight, and not the lifting itself. Some of us could, of course, lift a heavy weight even without such training. However, we'd risk hurting our back, because although we might possess the brute strength, we do not possess the skill. Lifting heavy weights correctly is an action in that it is a physical activity we are choosing to execute, but it is also an expression of something beyond the action — it is the expression of an attained knowledge: that of how to lift heavy weights appropriately (excellently).

This is why the Stoic philosophers don't describe Virtue as being something you *do*. What you do is a manifestation of who you are, and in Stoicism either you are virtuous or you are not. If you are virtuous, you are virtuous all the time, not only on occasion or by accident.

How, then, does a person who is virtuous all the time behave? Let's find out in the next chapter, where we discuss the Stoic sage.

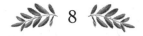

8

THE STOIC SAGE

I do not put the sage in a separate class from the rest of humankind, and neither do I eliminate pain and grief from him as if he were some sort of rock, not susceptible to any feeling.

— SENECA THE YOUNGER, *Letter to Lucilius* 71.27

STOIC SAGES ARE VIRTUOUS. This means that they are people of excellent character — they are incapable of making a *moral* mistake, but they are neither all-knowing nor perfect. Those who are not yet sages but who are traveling along the Stoic path are prokoptôntes. They are works in progress, which, unfortunately, means that they are still vicious, at least in the strictly Stoic sense of the word.

You might be thinking, "Certainly someone who has been practicing Stoicism for a long time, but who isn't yet a sage, must be, at least, a little bit more virtuous than someone who has only just started practicing Stoicism or who has no interest in Stoicism at all."

But such thoughts are a misunderstanding of core Stoic ideas. You are either virtuous or you are not. If you are only a little bit unjust, then you are still unjust. Think of it like a puzzle. A puzzle is not complete until all the pieces are correctly placed. If all the pieces but one are correctly placed, the puzzle is not finished. An incomplete puzzle can be further from, or nearer to, completion, but a completed puzzle exists in only one state: with all the pieces correctly placed.

The Stoics also teach the "Unity of Virtue." They believe that no single Virtue (e.g., Courage) can be expressed without mastery of all the other Virtues (Wisdom, Temperance, and Justice). For example, if you were a judge who lacked the courage to convict someone, you could hardly be referred to as "just." Indeed, your cowardice would skew your reasoning and ruin your ability to judge fairly. Likewise, you could hardly be considered wise if you had no self-control over your thoughts and actions, and so on. Remember that Virtue is an internal characteristic that is present in an individual who never acts or thinks inappropriately or immorally. Such an individual would never hold attitudes that were inappropriate or immoral either. They wouldn't assent to incorrect impressions or mistake what was within their control for what wasn't within their control.

Again, this doesn't mean that such a person — the Stoic sage — knows everything. Complete knowledge of everything that exists is not humanly possible. They aren't perfect at everything either, for another characteristic of the sage is that they know which domains are (or are not) appropriate for them to venture into (physically or intellectually). For example, a particular sage might be terrible at horseback riding, but this is why they would never advise on how best to ride a horse until they knew how to ride excellently. If they ever wanted to know how to ride a horse, they would lean on their character to identify who would be an excellent teacher and then set about learning the skill from that teacher. They wouldn't shy away from learning just because they don't presently know anything about riding horses. Likewise, a sage may know little about advanced science or mathematics, and this is why they would avoid teaching a class on these subjects until they had obtained the necessary information and training to teach these subjects well.

Entering the science classroom as a teacher when you don't know enough science to teach it is inappropriate. Entering the science classroom as a student, when you don't know enough to teach science, is entirely appropriate. A sage, like everyone else, can occupy multiple roles in their lifetime, and the role of student could easily be one of them.

Maybe you are now asking, "Has a virtuous person ever even existed?"

The ancient Stoics are said to have believed that sagehood was achievable in practice, not just in theory. However, they also wrote that sages were as rare as the phoenix — which makes them exceedingly rare. Seneca the Younger believed that the Stoic Roman general and statesman Cato the Younger was a sage. Others pointed to Socrates. However, arguing as to whether a sage can exist — and if one did or does, who they might be — is to miss the point. After all, a medical doctor has in their mind's eye an idea of a perfectly healthy person. That doesn't mean the doctor has ever seen someone who fits that description, or that such a person even exists. The point is that they approach their clinical work *as if* perfect health exists and can be achieved. The same holds true for excellence of character. The sage might not actually exist, but why not have the ideal sage in your mind's eye as you monitor your thoughts and execute your actions during any given moment?

Stoicism is a lifelong practice of incremental progress toward a destination that we may never reach. However, the same holds true for many journeys. You may set out to be a world-class neurosurgeon, but that destination may not actually exist for you — and yet that doesn't mean you shouldn't try. For if you never try, you certainly will never become one! You may also miss out on discovering that while you aren't the best neurosurgeon, you are a world-class psychologist — and there is nothing wrong with opening those doors instead.

In the next chapter, we switch gears and talk about the communal aspect of Stoicism. While the Stoic path is traveled by individuals, Stoicism isn't an individualistic or lone-wolf philosophy or pursuit.

THE CIRCLES OF CONCERN

Let this verse be in your heart and in your mouth: I am a human being, I regard nothing human as foreign to me. Let us hold things in common, as we are born for the common good.

— SENECA THE YOUNGER, *Letters to Lucilius* 95.53

THE STOICS ARE COSMOPOLITANS, meaning they believe that all Earth's inhabitants are citizens of the same singular community (or "world city"). They also believe that we have a responsibility to serve that community in whatever ways we are fit to do so.

Our obligations to each other are captured by the Stoic Hierocles's "Circles of Concern." These are a set of concentric circles, labeled from the center out in the following order: "self," "family," "friends," "community," and "humanity." Hierocles's circles were extended in 2018 by Kai Whiting, Leonidas Konstantakos, and others[1] to include the Earth, in order to reflect our contemporary understanding of the nonhuman world (animals, plants, and the other living and nonliving elements of the planet).

The self is at the center of the Circles of Concern for reasons similar to the reasons why, in the event of low cabin pressure on a commercial flight, we are instructed to put on our own oxygen masks before helping others with theirs; if we are not healthy versions of ourselves, we cannot help others to become healthier versions of themselves.

The ancient Stoics taught that we should aim to draw each of the Circles of Concern inward toward the self. In this conscious act, we bring the whole of humanity closer to our sense of self until we can recognize ourselves in all of humanity and all of humanity in ourselves. This is not to say that Stoics are called to treat everyone in exactly the same way — as if all people were identical in their beliefs, behaviors, interests, or expectations. It would certainly be inappropriate (and unwise) to treat our best friend's spouse the same way we treat our own! It would also be foolish to treat our own children like we would treat a stranger's children.

The conceptualization of the Stoic Circles of Concern expresses two key convictions within Stoicism. First, we humans naturally feel a more direct or pressing connection toward some people (such as family and friends) than we do toward others. Second, all human beings should be able to participate in our communities as world citizens, regardless of their gender, ethnicity, sexuality, country of origin, or financial status.

The Roman emperor Marcus Aurelius alluded to this cosmopolitan ideal when he wrote, in what is now known as *Meditations* (11.8), that "a man separates himself from his neighbor by his own hatred or rejection, not realizing that he has thereby severed himself from the wider society of fellow citizens."

As we work to bring people closer to our center, our friends become family, members of our community become our friends, and everyone, along with planet Earth and its nonhuman inhabitants, is understood to share a deep connection with us: the *Logos* (more on this in chapter 13).

Only sages can bring all the circles neatly into the self. For the rest of us, becoming more cosmopolitan in our outlook is an ongoing effort. When we are paying proper attention to the state of our mind, while thinking and acting appropriately, we are necessarily (as prosocial beings) pulling people closer toward us and under our wing.

Lastly, and importantly, the concept of the Circles of Concern isn't an invitation to have five hundred "internet friends" or "fans" whom we cannot hope to know, but rather a conscious and careful decision to cultivate connections with people we can truly journey alongside. The exact way in which we bring the circles inward, and the kinds of people we choose to bring closest, will depend heavily on our social roles. It is to these, then, and therefore to Stoic role ethics, that we now turn.

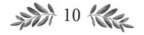

ROLES AND THE COSMOPOLIS

If someone ordered a singer in a chorus to "know himself," would he not attend to the order by paying attention both to his fellow chorus members and to harmonizing with them? — Yes — And so for a sailor? Or a soldier?

— EPICTETUS, *Fragment* 1

SERVICE TO THE COSMOPOLIS is a core part of Stoicism. All of us, in accordance with our social roles, are called to do our part as world citizens. Some of what we do will be in the capacity of a familial role (e.g., parent or grandparent). Other times, it will depend on our occupation, geographical location, or even hobbies.

In Stoicism, a role is something like a duty or responsibility that has been assigned to us. The

Stoic Panaetius defined our duties to one another relative to these:

1. our humanity
2. our personality
3. our social standing
4. our personal choices (such as our chosen career)

Roles can be assigned in several different ways. All of us share one primary role: that of a human being. This is our most important role, and no subsequent role can contradict our calling as a human being to think and act with Virtue in mind. As Epictetus put it, "Humans are first and foremost citizens of the cosmos" (*Discourses* 1.9.2).

In this respect, we cannot, while acting rationally, put our family's well-being before that of humanity's. In fact, to do so would be a contradiction in terms, as detaching ourselves from the cosmopolis for the sake of our family can only ever bring us misery to the detriment of our family! Perhaps this sounds contradictory. You may be thinking, "If I'm at the center of the circles, and my family is the next circle out, how could I ever prioritize broader humanity or planetary concerns over my own family?"

Again, if you're thinking critically, this is something you should absolutely be asking yourself. If we imagine the Circles of Concern as a flat disc, and then pinch the center of that disc and pull it up, turning it into a conical pyramid of rings, we have the same information but presented differently. We like to call this new image the Pyramid of Concern. The self is on top, and family the next ring down; further down still, there is the whole of humanity, supported by the Earth. Viewing our relationships with others in this way means that

THE PYRAMID OF CONCERN

it becomes easier to see that if the base is allowed to crumble, then everything above is put at risk of ruin. To care for the self at the top of this pyramid, one must care about, and care for, the base of the pyramid. One must care about humanity and the planet upon which we all live.

When it comes to what we might see as potential trade-offs, the sage understands that there are no *moral* compromises. But what about other types of compromises, such as deciding whether to reduce the amount of time you spend with your family in order to fulfill a commitment to a neighbor? In all cases, we are called to do what is reasonable in the present moment, and not what is ideal according to, for example, a religious or political ideology.

Imagine that your neighbor knocks on your door requesting help. They've lost their dog; it dug under their fence and escaped. You are aware that joining them will, inevitably, reduce the time you have to, say, bathe your youngest child (and let's imagine you were about to do that). Reason will tell you whether you should prioritize bath time or help your neighbor. To work out which choice is appropriate, given your seemingly conflicting roles as both parent and neighbor, you would need to consider things like these:

- Who else can help search for my neighbor's lost dog right now?
- Who else can bathe my child?
- Could I perhaps bathe my child later today, or even tomorrow?

If the answer to the first question is "No one else can help, I am the only one available," and the answer to the second one is "My spouse can do it," and the answer to the last one is "Yes, my spouse could bathe our child in an hour," then, arguably, it becomes unreasonable not to help your neighbor. However, if your spouse were ill to the point that they were unable to care for your child, then what is reasonable changes. As we have already said, context matters.

The Stoics were adamant that no virtuous person's role can conflict with any of their other roles. In practice this means, for example, that the good neighbor must *necessarily* act out their human duty to develop their individual nature, including their strengths, talents, and abilities, for the common good by helping their neighbors and caring for their neighborhood. This reality is what Marcus Aurelius reminds himself of when he states, in *Meditations* 6.54, "What cannot be good for the beehive cannot be good for the bee." In other words, no bee can benefit from the destruction of their hive.

All roles, no matter how they came to be assigned (or what they are), carry with them certain responsibilities. Stoics take fulfilling these responsibilities seriously and stress the importance of learning how to undertake them appropriately, as to fail to do so would speak negatively of their character.

Roles can be assigned to us in many ways. One way is as the result of the choices we make. For example, we may have a romantic relationship with someone and, nine months later, find ourselves in the role of mother or father. Another way could be through our career, our government, or our friendships. For example, we can fill the role of chef, US taxpayer, or best friend. We may also be a son or daughter, but how does one go about being a good son or daughter? How does one appropriately fill any role?

While the ancient Stoics advocated for role models (which is why they were also big on mentorship), they also knew that no two people's roles are identical. How you are personally called to fulfill your role as a son or daughter, for example, will necessarily be different from how your brothers and/or sisters are called to fulfill their similar familial roles. If you live locally to your parents and your sibling lives abroad, then it becomes obvious why, despite sharing the same parents, you will live out your respective roles as your parents' children very differently. Outside of understanding that Virtue is the only good, there is no *one* way to practice Stoicism and there is no *one* path to sagehood. There is no one path to being a good parent, son, daughter, or friend either!

Stoicism, like grammar, is a framework. Once you decide to write a letter in English, English grammar will tell you how to structure the letter accordingly. However, grammar won't help you with content. You must decide what kind of letter you want to write. In the same way, you must decide the kind of life you want to live. As Epictetus states (in *Discourses* 1.1), "If you're writing to a friend, grammar will tell you what letters you ought to choose, but as to whether or not you ought to write to your friend, grammar won't tell you that."

If you decide that you want to live a life centered on making progress toward Virtue, then Stoicism will point you in the general direction. However, Stoicism won't tell you how many times you need to rest along the journey or which walking shoes work best for your feet!

How can this be? How can a philosophy that seems so specific and intentional not have a rule book a meter thick?

The answer to that question is that there is but one rule — or, more appropriately, one law — that the Stoics insist we must abide by: Natural Law, the rational and purposeful order of the cosmos. It is this law, and not any particular fact, that dictates to us what the appropriate actions are in whichever situation we might find ourselves. It is also this law that led the Stoics to establish that Virtue is the only good; that the universe is benevolent; that reality is rooted in an observable, immanent God (see chapter 12); and that we are called to live according to Nature (both our own nature and that of the natural world).

This belief can be explained in the following manner: If you drop an apple from your roof, it will fall to the ground and not travel upward, because gravity dictates that this is the way objects fall. Likewise, when you identify Virtue as the only good (and the only thing worthy of pursuing), regardless of circumstances, you are simply abiding by Natural Law. Expecting to flourish while behaving poorly is like expecting an apple to fly upward when you drop it from your roof. To put this more directly, when you identify Virtue as the only good, and make an effort to work toward cultivating it in your own character, you are doing what a human being is *supposed* to do.

11

EMOTIONS

Believe me, true joy is a serious matter....
Look to your real good and rejoice in what is
yours. What is it that is yours? Yourself; the
best part of you.

— SENECA THE YOUNGER, *Letters to Lucilius* 23.4, 23.6

THE WORD *STOICISM* (uppercase *S*) is the Stoic philosophy we've been discussing up until now. Stoicism is different from stoicism (lowercase *s*). This easy-to-miss uppercase/lowercase distinction is one you will need to pay close attention to in this chapter. The word *stoicism* (lowercase *s*), as understood in the generic sense, is used to describe a seemingly cold and aloof response or attitude toward life. It is also strongly linked with masculine traits and is often seen as something negative, even "toxic." This is unfortunate, because there are times when being stoic is helpful. If you're a combat medic, for example, how emotional can you be on a battlefield before you can no longer perform your job well?

The contemporary Stoic author Jonathan Church offers an insightful view on how stoicism (lowercase *s*) helped him navigate his brain cancer diagnosis. Specifically, he states,

> As the neuro-oncologist informed me during a post-surgical consultation…, it's impossible to remove every cancerous cell.… During this ordeal, not once have I cried. Not once have I felt depressed, anxious, or out of sorts. Not once have I felt a need to seek therapeutic help. On the morning of surgery, I worried more about losing cognitive abilities if the surgery went awry than I did about death. One of my sisters commented that I was so calm she thought the doctors must have given me Valium. I was, in a word, stoic.…I have managed to develop a healthy perspective about brain cancer, which has helped me continue to live a happy and productive life and not succumb to anxiety and depression. I have stoicism to thank. I touched on this before in an essay on why I am a man who chooses not to cry. I argued that emotional restraint is not the same as emotional repression.[1]

Stoicism (uppercase *S*), the philosophy, is not about being cold and unemotional. We have already discussed the prosocial nature of a properly functioning human and the call to bring other people into our inner Circles of Concern. These core elements of Stoic philosophy distinguish it from stoicism as a way of living. However, and as discussed above (via the combat medic and following a cancer diagnosis), a Stoic may be called, at times, to behave stoically. Context is key, and of course, there are times when a stoic attitude is completely inappropriate.

One of the reasons why some people, since ancient times, have assumed that Stoics advocate for permanent stoicism is because they are called to pay a great deal of attention to their character. This necessitates that they constantly monitor and measure their emotional responses. It is not for no reason that we might describe an enraged person as someone who has "lost their mind." And if we lose our mind (Stoically speaking, the *hegemonikon*, the "ruling faculty of the soul"), then we lose the only thing we truly possess (our power of reason, our ability to make rational choices).

Some people make the mistake of thinking that the sage (the ideal Stoic) is so at ease with themselves and others that they don't need, or even experience, emotions. This is as untrue as it is unreasonable. A calm and balanced demeanor doesn't mean an unfeeling one. Instead, it refers to a demeanor that doesn't succumb to the extreme emotions that can be triggered when a person fails to recognize Virtue as the only good and mistakes a preferred indifferent as something good or a dispreferred indifferent as something bad.

So, what does the sage feel? They feel the good emotions (*eupatheiai*). As Margaret Graver states, "These include awe and reverence, certain forms of joy and gladness, certain particular kinds of love and friendship, and some powerful types of longing or wishing."[2]

A more in-depth investigation of the positive emotions tells us that the sage experiences enjoyment and cheerfulness. They're also welcoming and good-willed. They experience erotic love, when it is tied to the prospect of friendship, beauty, and the common good of the cosmopolis (as opposed to something lustful or merely pleasure-oriented). They are pious, are cautious in their assents (judgments), and are careful in their moral conduct.

What is absent in the sage's emotions? The *pathê* (negative emotions). These include spite, hatred, rage, envy, pity, nonbodily fear responses, panic, anguish, and misery, to name a few. The truly balanced character has no need for such emotions, because they recognize that these emotions do not help in the cultivation and maintenance of a good character. On the contrary, negative emotions are expressed when we assent to the false impression that, for example, losing a prized indifferent (e.g., a well-paying job) is something we should fear or panic over. That said, this doesn't mean we shouldn't react at all. Indeed, the Stoics invite a measured reaction rooted in the understanding that neither fear nor panic will, to continue the well-paying job example, help us get our job back or, alternatively, help us find a new one. It is the measured response and not the panicked one that enhances the possibility of our finding a new job. In addition, and as we discussed in chapter 3, it is rational, all things being equal, to prefer gainful employment over long-term unemployment.

When we begin our Stoic journey, we are not embarking on the process of becoming emotionless creatures. Neither are we encouraged by the Stoics to view the world through rose-colored glasses so that we may overlook or underplay life's difficulties. Instead, we are learning to take those steps that allow us to work through our negative emotions until, one day, we can leave them behind. In fact, the ancient Stoics often advocated for the imagining of the worst-case scenario so that the prokoptôn could come to terms with it rather than be overcome by it.

At the same time, we are called to experience good emotions because these enable us to fully flourish as human beings. These emotions also make life enjoyable and bring benefit to others; in short, they allow us to live our humanity to the fullest.

THE STOIC GOD

Remember that you are an actor in a drama, which is as the playwright wishes; if the playwright wishes it short, it will be short; if long, then long; if the playwright wishes you to play a beggar, it is assigned to you in order that you good-naturedly play even that role; and similarly if you are assigned to play a disabled person, a public official, or a layperson. For this is what is yours: to finely play the role that is given; but to select itself is the role of the divine playwright.

— EPICTETUS, *The Encheiridion* 17

STOICISM DOES NOT MEET the contemporary definition of a "religion," but it does have a not-insignificant degree of, let's say, religiousness or spirituality associated with it. After all, the ancient Stoics *did* believe in God, sometimes referring to God as Zeus. They also believed in the concept of divine providence, going so far as to suggest that the cosmos is ordered by the divine creative fire (the Logos) and animated by the divine breath (*pneuma*). The Stoic God was providential but not personal in the sense of bestowing miracles upon favorite tribes or individuals.

For many people today, including those who call themselves "Stoic," the word *God* can be a loaded word. Perhaps this is unsurprising, given that several people who now walk the Stoic path found it after growing weary and wary of the God of their upbringing. In such cases, the Stoic God is often seen as an unwelcome and unnecessary intrusion into a life free from the religious rules and values they long grappled with and, happily, left behind.

Other contemporary Stoics may be nested in their religion and have a very positive association with the word *God*. However, they may feel equally uncomfortable with the Stoic God, as engaging with religious ideas outside of their chosen faith can put them in an awkward position. Some contemporary Stoics, especially those who follow an Abrahamic religion, may even feel that a belief in the Stoic God is a betrayal of the one "true" God and an unhelpful diversion away from "eternal salvation" or the "right path."

This is not a new problem. Indeed, the founding father of Neostoicism, Justus Lipsius, faced the same issue in the mid-1500s. Neostoicism was a movement that incorporated aspects of Christian metaphysics and ethics into a Stoic framework. Yet Lipsius's incoherent hybrid was something he ultimately rejected on his deathbed, in favor of traditional Christianity, after much intellectual wrangling and suffering brought on by cognitive dissonance (the holding of two contradictory beliefs at the same time). It seems that putting his faith in the Stoic God was a bridge too far, and ultimately it was a risk Lipsius was not willing to take for the sake of his mortal soul.

Regardless of which side of the fence you are on (if any), when it comes to your own religious views, you are perhaps now asking yourself, "Do I need to believe in the Stoic God in order to practice Stoicism?"

This is both a contentious and a complicated question to answer, but it is not something we, as authors — or as practitioners of Stoicism ourselves, for that matter — should sweep under the rug.

Remember that the Stoics claim Virtue to be the only good. This claim in Stoicism is what John 3:16 of the New Testament is to Christianity.[1] By definition, you cannot be a Christian if you do not believe in Christ as your Lord and savior (Muslims, for instance, believe that Jesus is the Messiah but *not* their Lord and savior[2]). By the same token, one cannot be a Stoic if one does not believe that Virtue is the only good. If we were to believe that Virtue was simply the highest good, we could be Aristotelians but not Stoics.

Believing that Virtue is the only good *is* a faith-based claim — and we use "faith" here not in an ecclesiastic sense, but in a "this can't be proved in a court of law or a science lab" sense. If you believe Virtue is the only good, you are taking a leap of faith or, if you prefer, you are trusting the ancient Stoics' argument for Natural Law (see chapter 10).

So, must we believe in the Stoic God in order to call ourselves Stoics?

Unequivocally, no. You do not have to believe in the Stoic God in order to consider yourself a Stoic.

However, everything in Stoicism is built on the Stoic conceptualization of God. So, for example, if you believe Virtue is the only good, the logical justification for that claim (according to the ancient Stoics) rests on the metaphorical shoulders of the Stoic God. This is because the Stoics' conceptualization of God, rooted in the rational observation of nature, was one of their key premises and, consequently, how they *reasoned themselves* to their views on Virtue. For the ancient Stoics (not to mention a sizable contingent of contemporary ones), then, to deny the Stoic God is like standing on the roof of your home and denying the existence of the walls that hold it up.

So, no, you do not have to believe in the Stoic God in order to call yourself a Stoic, but a sort of cognitive dissonance is created when you claim that Virtue is the only good while, at the same time, brushing Stoic physics and logic off as unimportant (we'll talk about these two in chapter 15).

Given what we have just said, a better question than "Do I need to believe in the Stoic God in order to practice Stoicism?" is "What am I attempting to get out of Stoicism, and does the Stoic God add any value to my practice?"

Let's now explore the Stoic conceptualization of God in more detail.

The Stoics viewed God as an animal. Not as a panda, nor a lion, nor an eagle, but as *the universe.* This may, at first pass, seem absurd; but is it? Is it so strange to consider the universe as a kind of animal with various life-sustaining processes and constituent parts? Humans have arms and legs. The universe has planets, stars, and black holes. It also has rocks, trees, and people. Yes, we too, according to the ancient Stoics, form part of the universe. We too make up some of that animal's anatomy.

Reason (Logos) is the animal's physical mind-soul and the universal connection between all beings (including nonliving things like rocks). You can also view the Logos as the universe's creative life force. One that is entirely rational, orderly, and benevolent because it gives every being an opportunity to live according to their own nature. When we choose not to live with Virtue in mind, Marcus Aurelius (in *Meditations* 2.16) says we become like an abscess on the universe's body — and who willingly wants to be a painful collection of pus? Who wants to be a burden instead of a building block?

Might the Stoics' conceptualization of God help us remember exactly what we are and remind us of our capacity to cultivate a good character?

In our opinion, the Stoic God is an interesting conception of the Divine because it is a wholly natural one. The "philosophical proofs" for the Stoic God were not arrived at through superstition or through a desire to enter heaven or escape hell (neither exist in Stoic theology). Instead, the Stoics saw God as a fact whose signs and effects can be perceived by the senses. Epictetus asserts this in *Discourses* 1.16 (as translated by George Long):

> But now we, instead of being thankful that
> we need not take the same care of animals
> as of ourselves, complain of God on our

own account; and yet, in the name of Zeus and the gods, any one thing of those which exist would be enough to make a man perceive the providence of God, at least a man who is modest and grateful. And speak not to me now of the great things, but only of this, that milk is produced from grass, and cheese from milk, and wool from skins. Who made these things or devised them? No one, you say. O amazing shamelessness and stupidity!

For me (Tanner), the Stoic God is something not worth arguing over. Stoicism requires that we believe Virtue is the only good. This, itself, is an unprovable claim and, in my eyes, a claim of faith or trust in the ancient Stoic position. Whether or not someone doubles down on this claim by choosing to believe in the Stoic God, they are still committing themselves to believing *something* on faith. This, in my opinion, is a fundamental part of growing up: choosing to believe in something that makes sense to you. For me, that's the goodness of Virtue and the pursuit of it through the ethical and logical branches of Stoicism. I don't spend much time thinking about the Stoic God, and if I ever change that, I won't allow anything other than the *benefits* of choosing to believe in the Stoic

God — how doing so might improve my life and the lives of those in my circles of concern — to determine whether that choice is worthwhile or not. I certainly won't allow other people's feelings about my choice to determine whether or not I choose to change it.

For me (Kai), Stoicism without God is not Stoic philosophy but rather a Stoic-influenced practice that leaves too many inconsistencies for me to be comfortable with as an academic who studies and lives his life according to Stoic principles. Does that mean I think that Stoic concepts without God are useless to a person who wants to improve their life? Not at all. For me, however, Stoicism isn't Stoicism if we ignore or outrightly reject the Stoic God.

At the risk of stating the obvious, both of us are philosophers of Stoicism who also identify as Stoics, and we don't agree with each other on the importance of the Stoic God. This means you can agree with either of us (or neither of us) and still call yourself a Stoic. There's no dogmatic orthodoxy here, and that's a very liberating thing indeed for people who are exploring Stoicism as their potential life philosophy.

13

LIVE IN ACCORDANCE WITH NATURE

Whatever is done in accordance with Nature is rightly done.

— EPICTETUS, *Discourses* 1.11.5

"LIVE IN ACCORDANCE WITH NATURE" is one of the most repeated phrases in Stoicism — but what does it mean, and how central is it to adopting Stoicism as a life philosophy?

Fundamentally, living according to Nature is about understanding and responding to the reality of where you are (both figuratively and geographically) and undertaking your roles and responsibilities in line with that reality. Living according to Nature, then, is as much about knowing yourself (a maxim that Stoicism's founder, Zeno of Citium, had to agree to when visiting the Oracle of Delphi) as it is about trying to understand the world around you.

Posidonius is a prime example of a Stoic who tried to understand the mind of God in his effort to live according to Nature. The way in which he did it, through meticulous observations of the natural world, also spoke to his own nature and the workings of his inquisitive mind.

As Kai Whiting and Leonidas Konstantakos state in their book *Being Better: Stoicism for a World Worth Living In*, "Posidonius accepted that the capacity for rationality allowed humans to better understand and cooperate with the cosmos; he also saw that most people gave in too easily to their base desires and the 'emotional pulls' of their own idiosyncratic nature. He believed this behavior made them miserable because in falling back into Vice — cowardice, injustice, greed, and ignorance — they misaligned themselves with God's own nature and providential purposes."

In short, what Posidonius observed was a failure of humans to live according to their own nature and to maintain a balance with Nature. To "live according to Nature" is to live in harmony with the natural world, with the exact way we do so being dependent upon many factors, including our age, where we live, our occupation, and our personal preferences.

If we are Christian, for example, we might wish to consider how we can make our place of worship more environmentally friendly — perhaps by making the grounds a more welcoming habitat for local fauna and flora. If we are a grandparent, perhaps we could take our grandchildren for walks in nature so they can grow to have an appreciation of it. If we are a dog owner, we can think carefully about what our dog eats and wears, and where it walks — as all of these elements have an impact on the environment.

As Stoics, we draw the "environment" part of the Circle of Concern inward when we consider and care for the Earth. For how could the sage advocate for taking more than they need, or for the wanton or careless destruction of the planet, where everyone they know lives and breathes?

Living according to Nature is also to submit to Divine Reason, although the way we do so is dependent upon who we are (see chapter 10). Living according to Nature is not an invitation to subject yourself to the capricious whims of a jealous God. Nor is it an invitation to lord your personal beliefs over others — those who live according to Nature recognize that they belong to the universal community of Reason, not a special tribe of chosen people.

Living according to Nature is also about living excellently. For humans, as prosocial creatures, living excellently is living virtuously and contributing to the common good. Living excellently culminates in the cultivation of a character that is incapable of making a moral mistake. It is about knowing what is good and what is bad and knowing how to choose that which is neither good nor bad (Stoic indifferents) appropriately, so you build up, rather than break down and destroy, your character.

The sage is completely in tune with Nature. They understand their role as perfectly as any human can, and they fulfill it completely. They are able to bring each Circle of Concern in upon the previous one, until they fully see themselves in humanity and humanity in themselves. They are totally rooted in the Logos and at ease with themselves and all others, including the natural world. This is what it means to live according to Nature. This is what it means to flourish.

14

FATE

Lead me Zeus, and thou O Destiny. Lead me wherever your laws assign me.... Fate guides the willing but drags the unwilling.

— CLEANTHES, *Hymn to Zeus*

THE WAY WE ENVISION "good luck" and "bad luck" today would have been completely alien to the ancient Stoics and their understanding of Fate and the way the world works. Under the Stoic worldview, nothing is truly random. Instead, everything is the unfolding of cause and effect as part of the natural order of things. We are very much a part of this order, and in this way Fate happens *through us*, not *to us*.

Stoicism offers a famous example, associated with Zeno of Citium and other Stoic figures: "When a dog is tied to a cart, if it wants to follow it is pulled and follows, making its spontaneous act coincide with necessity, but if it does not want to follow it will be compelled in any case. So it is with men [and women] too: even if they do not want to, they will be compelled in any case to follow what is destined."[1]

We may not have a choice in the direction we are being taken, but how we choose to direct our steps, as we go in that direction, remains up to us. There is never a matter in Stoicism in which we have no choice. Even where we seemingly have but one choice, we can choose to make that choice willingly or unwillingly. As John Sellars states, "It may be that I will not, and cannot, act other than I do. Yet the act is still mine...and not forced upon me."[2]

Another way of thinking about the Stoic concept of Fate is to imagine ourselves in a canoe, journeying down a river. In our hands is a paddle. This paddle gives us a degree of freedom to navigate the river (it's like the rope tied to the dog cart), freedom that can increase if we learn to use it well. In this regard, the paddle represents our agency. We can choose to take the left (or right) option at the fork in the river, and we can move closer to or further away from the canoes of others who are also paddling along. How we use the paddle represents our character. Our ability to make the best use of it will depend on the skills we have acquired and the mindset we have worked to develop (remember that a virtuous character is something we cultivate).

We could, of course, throw away our paddle, deciding to do nothing but allow Fate to carry us. This effectively removes any degree of freedom we might have otherwise had to navigate the river. After we make such a decision, Fate can only ever happen *to* us and not *through* us. In a sense, we have thrown our hands up into the air and given up. Of course, even if we choose to keep ahold of our paddle, and learn to use it well, we are still restricted in what that paddle enables us to control. But again, this doesn't mean we shouldn't keep paddling, since by paddling we can still influence our journey.

The river itself is our environment, and it sets certain boundaries and limitations. For instance, we have next to no control over the nature of the riverbanks and the riverbed. We must simply navigate them. The river's flow represents time. Once we make decisions, we cannot undo them but must continue in anticipation of our next challenge, and thus our next choice. We can face this either willingly or unwillingly. We can focus on our past mistakes — maybe we nearly hit some rocks a few miles back — and be fearful of what may lie ahead, or we can do our best to navigate what comes with determination and the skilled sweeps of our paddle.

The Stoic view of how to navigate this river, and, consequently, how to conceptualize the idea of Fate, is to accept what control we lack and to utilize what control or influence we possess.

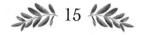

15

STOIC PHYSICS AND LOGIC

Suppose you said to me, "I don't know whether your argument is valid or invalid," and when I made use of some ambiguous term, you said, "Draw the distinction," I would lose patience with you and reply, "But there is a more urgent need." That is the reason, I fancy, why philosophers begin with logic, just as, when measuring grain, one begins by examining the measure.

— EPICTETUS, *Discourses* 1.17.5–6

STOICISM, AT ITS CORE, is made up of three parts: physics, logic, and ethics. We have spent much of this short book talking about Stoic ethics by discussing the nature of Virtue, Vice, good and evil, indifferents and the art of selecting them, the sage, the prokoptôn, and our emotions. Indeed, the ethics portion of Stoicism is largely responsible for the renewed interest in the philosophy we've seen since 2010 and gets the lion's share of attention in contemporary Stoic circles (with the College of Stoic Philosophers, and their focus on all aspects of Stoic philosophy, being a notable exception).

This is truly unfortunate because, as Julia Annas states, being a good Stoic requires more than mastering the ethical part.[1] It also requires a firm grounding in Stoic physics and logic. In fact, the ancient Stoics held that a practitioner had to understand logic before they could progress to the ethics, and then the physics.

The Stoic use of the word *physics* doesn't mean physics as we understand it today (e.g., the study of the laws of gravity and thermodynamics). Rather, it refers to the way in which the world works, and so it also involves things that today we would more readily call Biology or Natural Philosophy. As we have discussed in previous chapters, the Stoics took God as a fundamentally observable fact of reality and not as a personal God of faith like the God of Abraham. Belief in God was simply an acknowledgment of what was true, and thus a fundamental component of Stoic physics.

A. A. Long states that Stoic ethics are rooted in, even parasitical on, Stoic physics.[2] Meaning that the ethics make no sense if the Stoic conception of the world (and so God) is ignored or rejected. Indeed, the claim that Virtue is the only good is fundamentally tied to the idea that God is benevolent.

The call to live according to Nature is, likewise, tied to Divine Reason (the Logos), and tied to the idea that the whole universe is imbued by a rationality that we are called upon not only to appreciate but also to actively model in our role as human beings.

Such arguments suggest that to strip the Stoic God from Stoic ethics is to leave more holes than substance. You might have some useful concepts you can apply to your life, but can this really be called Stoicism? Of course, when it comes to your personal journey into Stoicism, how you reconcile Stoic ideas about God with your own practice is entirely up to you.

We now turn our attention to Stoic logic, which encompasses formal reasoning via debate (the Socratic method), the study of language, the solving of formal logical puzzles, and the investigation of ambiguities and sophisms (clever but bad arguments that are typically used deliberately to deceive an audience).

Logic is seen by the Stoics as integral to obtaining the kind of knowledge that supports us in the cultivation of a good character. Logic is important because if we are continually drawing illogical conclusions, we are going to have a very warped view of the world and our role within it.

Let's take one aspect of logic: the ability to properly construct an argument, as highlighted by Epictetus's words in the quote at the beginning of this chapter. This kind of logic is tested in the Socratic method. In a nutshell, the Socratic method is the art of systematic, critical, and sincere questioning and answering to identify both the coherence and the trueness of a belief via the purposeful uncovering of contradictions.

When a group of people engages in dialogue with this goal in mind, everyone benefits because the exchange becomes about what is right, not about what is merely popular (or emotionally satisfying). It is done in the interest of the whole and not for the sole benefit of one tribe to the detriment of all others. It is also a way to test the nature of your character, and it helps you to form better-quality thoughts. Without logic we cannot hope to know what is true and to distinguish it from what is false. Instead, we will become blinded by ideas and practices that are not rooted in reason, such as nepotism and tribalism — to the obvious detriment to our character and the common good. We will also be misled by statements that seem true and arguments that seem sound but are, in fact, far from it (i.e., sophisms), and in general, we will become increasingly unable to distinguish between a valid argument and an invalid one.

As the Stoic-influenced Roman statesman Cicero explained in his works *Academica* and *De*

Finibus, logic provides a method of reasoning that guards against the assenting to incorrect impressions (the making of faulty judgments) and, thus, serves us on our journey to eudaimonia.

To understand the benefit of Stoic logic more plainly, we might try thinking of it as a form of grammar. If your grammar is very poor, you can still write a sentence, and that sentence may still convey its message sufficiently for others to understand it. However, if you string too many grammatically poor sentences together, into a book or a complicated set of instructions, then it becomes highly likely that something is going to get lost in translation. Imagine, for example, that your country's constitution contained dozens of grammatical errors. How might that impact a court of law's ability to make correct judgments on constitutional issues?

The ancient Stoics used logic to ensure that the opinions or conclusions they arrived at were "sound." That doesn't mean that two sages must have exactly the same opinion (in fact, they could have seemingly contradictory ones). However, it does mean that they will have arrived at their opinions in the same way: through logically sound reasoning. This reason isn't absent of emotion, but neither is it formed solely on the basis of how a sage feels. As a result, a sage's reason can be followed by other people who are, likewise, in the pursuit of truth and eager to judge things correctly. We might not be sages but we can certainly try to emulate their way of making decisions as we attempt to bring benefit to everyone and everything around us.

Another way the Stoics determined whether an argument, position, or opinion was sound or defensible was to construct it as a syllogism. A syllogism is a way of expressing a form of reasoning that uses two assumed or given propositions to draw a conclusion. The Stoic Chrysippus of Soli set about demonstrating that he could verify the validity of nearly all statements by analyzing them with five hypothetical arguments. For our brief purposes, here is a taste of the kind of logical arguments the Stoics proposed (although not under such names):

- *Ponendo ponens* (a rule of inference) — In layperson's terms, if the first statement is true, then the second statement must also be true. For example, if we know that if it rains, the uncovered ground will be wet, and we see that it is raining, then we can conclude that the uncovered ground will be wet. In other words, if something happens, then a result will follow. If we see the first thing happening, we can be sure the result will also happen.

- *Tollendo tollens* — In plain language, if the first statement is true then the second statement is also true, but if the second statement is shown to be false, then the first statement must, by definition, also be false. In other words, we can negate the first assumption by negating the second. For example, if a cake is baked, it will be ready to eat. If the cake is not ready to eat, then it must not have been baked. In still other words, if something happening would lead to a certain result, and we see that the result did not happen, then we can be sure the first thing did not happen. "Not A and therefore not B" or A is only possible if B.

All that being said, the point of this chapter is to explain the *importance* of logic in Stoicism, not to teach you the logical arguments of Stoicism in any great depth. So, to sum up, Stoic logic combines formula-based systematically constructed arguments with rhetoric skills to increase the likelihood that the statements we make, and subsequently the opinions we form or the conclusions we draw, are carefully thought through and reasonable.

How does that help us on a day-to-day basis? In short, it helps immensely! From how to know if we are getting a bargain in the supermarket, to which university course to select to achieve our educational aims, to what we, perhaps, should bear in mind when considering the kind of life partner we want. Approaching such things with a logical mind, rather than just based on how we feel at the time, can make life a lot easier. It's easy to believe we are in love with someone when we have butterflies in our stomach, and it's just as easy to believe that we no longer love a person when those butterflies disappear, *if* we rely solely on faulty logic that tells us that "butterflies in our stomach" is what love is. And surely, love is too important to base on feelings alone.

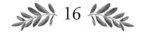

16

Stoicism in Summary

Our whistle-stop tour of Stoicism has come to an end, and we would like to leave you with a very brief summary of the main points we covered.

Zeno of Citium founded Stoicism in 300 BCE. He wanted his philosophy to be accessible to the masses. Therefore, he taught it in the open air of the Athenian marketplace, at the Stoa Poikile, or Painted Porch, which is what gave Stoicism its name.

Virtue is the inherent good nature of a person's character (should they possess it). It is "a form of expertise or skill," and "knowledge that shapes [a person's] whole personality and life."[1]

Virtue is the only good, and Vice is the only bad, but that doesn't mean that other things don't matter. Indeed, how we pursue or avoid indifferents speaks of our character.

Indifferents are things that can't guarantee us a good character nor prevent us from developing a good character. Some indifferents are preferred, while others are dispreferred. To distinguish indifferents, we use reason, paying particular attention to context and our social roles.

IMPRESSIONS ARE AMONG OUR INITIAL INTERPRETATIONS OF REALITY, and we must examine them closely before assenting to them, lest we go too far down the rabbit hole of believing falsehoods (which makes developing a virtuous character increasingly difficult).

THE DICHOTOMY OF CONTROL REMINDS US THAT SOME THINGS ARE WITHIN OUR ABILITY TO CONTROL OR INFLUENCE, while other things are not. Remembering this allows us, over time, to better manage our reactions to the things we have no control over. There are only three things we do have control over: our own thoughts, our own actions, and our own attitudes. Only these will have any effect on our moral character.

STOIC PROKOPTÔNTES ARE PRACTITIONERS OR STUDENTS OF STOICISM. Such people are on the path to sagehood, and they move toward eudaimonia when they undertake appropriate acts and hold appropriate thoughts and attitudes.

PROSOCHĒ IS THE ART/PRACTICE OF PAYING ATTENTION, of being vigilant over the state of our own mind (hegemonikon) for the sake of our character.

VIRTUE IS BINARY: you either have it or you don't. If you do, it means you completely embody the four Cardinal Virtues (Wisdom, Courage, Justice, and Temperance). If you don't, then you are still a work in progress.

THE STOIC SAGE IS THE IDEAL STOIC. Sages are of excellent character and are incapable of making moral mistakes.

THE CIRCLES OF CONCERN REMIND US OF OUR STOIC DUTY to bring people closer to us and to care for them as much as we care for ourselves. The Circles also remind us of the duty of care that we have toward animals, plants, and the planet.

ROLES DEFINE OUR RESPONSIBILITIES, whether they're assigned to us upon our birth (e.g., son or daughter), through our actions, through our personal preferences, by our employers, or by society. Our roles help us to answer the question "What is appropriate to be thinking and doing in this situation?" Our primary role is that of a human being.

STOICISM IS HIGHLY CONTEXTUAL. There's no one way to be a Stoic, no broad advice that can be applied in the exact same manner regardless of the situation you find yourself in. Instead, you must reason through your situation and decide what is appropriate right then and there, for you, given your social roles.

STOICS FEEL AND EXPRESS EMOTIONS; they're

not cold, unfeeling statues. However, they are careful when it comes to how they choose to react. As they progress toward eudaimonia, Stoics will naturally become less affected by the negative emotions (e.g., hatred and spite) and harness the positive ones — without the need for rose-colored glasses!

THERE IS A GOD IN STOICISM, best thought of as Nature, but you do not need to believe in the Stoic God to call yourself a Stoic or to find Stoicism beneficial. That said, Stoic ethics are rooted in the idea that there is a God and that such a God is benevolent and observable. The idea that Virtue is the only good rests on the metaphorical shoulders of the Stoic God.

LIVING IN ACCORDANCE WITH NATURE IS ABOUT LIVING EXCELLENTLY and submitting to Divine Reason.

THE STOICS BELIEVE FATE HAPPENS *THROUGH* US, not *to* us. Even if we feel that we have only one choice, we can always choose whether to make that choice willingly or unwillingly.

STOIC PHYSICS AND LOGIC ARE INSEPARABLE FROM STOIC PHILOSOPHY without introducing inconsistencies and holes in the underlying theory. Stoic physics is concerned with how the world is — this includes natural processes and the nature of God, as a universal and observable presence.

Stoic logic is the art of examining our reasoning. To progress along the path of eudaimonia and to achieve a flourishing life is a logical process, which requires logical thought.

EPILOGUE

WE HOPE THAT AFTER READING our book *What Is Stoicism?* you have a better understanding of Stoic philosophy — including its principles and practices. We also hope that you are in a better position to decide whether Stoicism, as a life philosophy, works for you.

Stoicism works for me (Tanner) because it underpins my life with a foundational code of ethics that I can turn to when I'm thinking through complicated issues. Its focus on Virtue has shifted the way I view the world and has made me a better person, a person with a character that seeks the knowledge that is Virtue. Finally, Stoicism provides me with a highly intellectual approach to understanding my duties and responsibilities to the cosmopolis, my friends, my family, and myself, something that has greatly improved the quality and enjoyability of my life.

Stoicism is my (Kai) philosophy of choice because I can use it both during times of ease and during times of hardship. When I cast my mind's eye on the sage, I find those few extra degrees of freedom and the strength and resilience to keep moving when my legs would otherwise give way.

Lastly, and from both of us (Tanner and Kai), whether Stoicism is for you or not, we wish you the absolute best on your journey of self-discovery and improvement. This is why we have left you a list of recommended reading at the end of this book!

ACKNOWLEDGMENTS

I (TANNER) WOULD LIKE TO THANK my community of listeners, readers, and supporters for their steadfast support of me and my work. Thanks to Will Johncock for his thoughtful feedback on very early drafts of this book; to Kai Whiting for encouraging me to write the book and agreeing to coauthor it with me; and finally, to my wife Ross and our son Cailean — I hope I've made you both proud.

I (Kai) would like to thank all those who played a key role in my life while I wrote this book — you know who you are: LGC, TGFCW, CCW, GLW, HMC, MJ, SEF, AP, LK, and, of course, TOC. Thank you, especially, to Dr. Leonidas Konstantakos for all our academic discussions and teaching sessions over the years — many of our conversations influenced the content of this book.

Together, we wish to thank Jason Gardner and his team, including Kristen Cashman, Cate Dapron, and Howie Severson, at New World Library for believing in us as authors and believing in our idea to write an accessible, non-watered-down introduction to Stoicism. We also thank Professor Aldo Dinucci for his help with the chapter "Stoic Physics and Logic." And we thank both Dr. Hanna Murray-Carlsson and LGC for their careful reading and feedback on the early drafts of *What Is Stoicism?* as well as for their helpful thoughts and suggestions throughout the writing process.

Glossary

WHILE WE DESIGNED THIS BOOK to be accessible, summarizing a philosophy is impossible without using at least some words that are generally unfamiliar to most people. For that reason, we thought a brief glossary of terms would be useful.

ASSENT: To accept that an impression (a judgment) is true.

CARDINAL VIRTUES: Wisdom, Courage, Temperance, and Justice. The four Virtues we must fully embody in order to attain a virtuous character.

CIRCLES OF CONCERN: The Stoic conceptual model as to how we should view and interact with the self, others, and the planet. Created by Hierocles the Stoic.

CITIUM: An ancient city on the island country of Cyprus. Modern-day Larnaca.

COSMOPOLIS: The universal world city.

COURAGE: One of the four Cardinal Virtues; the willingness to do what is right, even amid challenging circumstances.

DICHOTOMY OF CONTROL: A contemporary phrase used to describe the division between the things we are able to control and those we are not.

FATE: That which is destined to happen through you; that which is set to occur via the unfolding of natural events and processes.

HEGEMONIKON: The mind, the "ruling faculty of the soul."

HIEROCLES: An ancient Stoic philosopher from the second century CE. Author of the book *Elements of Ethics* and creator of the Stoic Circles of Concern.

IMPRESSION: A feeling or notion about a person, situation, or event that is something like an unproved theory; or a precursor to an assumption.

JUSTICE: One of the four Cardinal Virtues; fairness in our dealings with others and in the distribution of resources.

LOGOS: Universal divine reason that permeates the entire universe and connects all beings (biotic and abiotic).

ORACLE OF DELPHI: A prophesying woman who was sought out by all manner of citizens of the ancient world for her wisdom and advice.

PNEUMA: The divine breath; the force that gives life to all things.

PORTICO: A structure consisting of a roof supported by columns at regular intervals, typically attached to a building as a porch.

PROKOPTÔN (PROKOPTÔNTES): A person making progress along the Stoic path. The plural is prokoptôntes.

PROSOCHĒ: The practice of paying attention to your thoughts, actions, and attitudes so that you are better able to make appropriate decisions. Can also be seen as a kind of spiritual vigilance or mindfulness over the self.

SAGE: A virtuous person, one who is incapable of making a moral mistake.

SOCIAL ROLES: A collection of social or personal responsibilities/duties assigned by one's actions, by society, or by one's personal preferences. For some Stoics, God is the architect of these roles.

SOCRATIC METHOD: A way of engaging in dialogue with the aim of identifying the truth and reducing any tendencies toward faulty thinking, including false impressions and judgments.

SOPHISM: A clever but bad argument that is typically used to deliberately deceive an audience.

STOA POIKILE: "Painted Porch," the public walkway where Zeno of Citium taught Stoicism.

SUBORDINATE VIRTUES: Expressions of the Cardinal Virtues (e.g., piety).

TEMPERANCE: One of the four Cardinal Virtues; self-control, a measured response.

UNITY OF VIRTUE: The idea that Virtue can be possessed only once a person embodies all the Cardinal Virtues.

VICE (VICIOUSNESS): The absence of Virtue (see below).

VIRTUE: The inherent good moral nature of a person's character, should they possess it; "a form or expertise or skill," and "knowledge that shapes the whole personality and life."[1]

WISDOM: One of the four Cardinal Virtues; includes knowing what is good, what is bad, and what is neither good nor bad.

Notes

Chapter 3: Virtue and Indifferents

1   Lovingly borrowed from the film *National Lampoon's Christmas Vacation* (Warner Bros., 1989).

2   Scott Aikin and William O. Stephens, *Epictetus's Encheiridion, A New Translation and Guide to Stoic Ethics* (London: Bloomsbury Academic, 2023), 14.

3   William O. Stephens has written various scholarly papers defining and discussing the importance of the Stoic indifferents, particularly regarding their application to contemporary environmental challenges. His interpretation of the Stoic indifferents helped us write this chapter. One such example of his collaborative work with Kai is Kai Whiting, William O. Stephens, Edward Simpson, and Leonidas Konstantakos, "How Might a Stoic Eat in Accordance with Nature and 'Environmental Facts'?," *Journal of Agricultural and Environmental Ethics*, 33 (2020): 369–89.

Chapter 5: The Dichotomy of Control

1   Michael Tremblay, "What Many People Misunderstand about the Stoic Dichotomy of Control," *Modern Stoicism*, January 30, 2021, https://modernstoicism.com/what -many-people-misunderstand-about-the-stoic-dichotomy -of-control-by-michael-tremblay.

Chapter 6: The *Prokoptôn* and *Prosochē*

1   Christopher Fisher, "Prosochē: Illuminating the Path of
    the Prokoptōn," *Traditional Stoicism*, December 18, 2015,
    https://traditionalstoicism.com/wp-content/uploads
    /2018/03/Prosoche-Illuminating-the-Path-of-the
    -Prokopton.pdf.

2   Pierre Hadot, *What Is Ancient Philosophy?*, trans. Michael
    Chase (Cambridge, MA: Belknap Press, 2002), 138.

Chapter 9: The Circles of Concern

1   Kai Whiting, Leonidas Konstantakos, Angeles Carrasco,
    and Luis Gabriel Carmona, "Sustainable Development,
    Wellbeing and Material Consumption: A Stoic Perspec-
    tive," *Sustainability* 10, no. 2 (2018): 474.

Chapter 11: Emotions

1   Jonathan Church, "How My Toxic Stoicism Helped Me
    Cope with Brain Cancer," *Quillette*, January 23, 2019,
    https://quillette.com/2019/01/23/how-my-toxic-stoicism
    -helped-me-cope-with-brain-cancer.

2   Margaret Graver, *Stoicism and Emotion* (Chicago: Univer-
    sity of Chicago Press, 2007), 4.

Chapter 12: The Stoic God

1   "For God so loved the world that he gave his one and
    only Son, that whoever believes in him shall not perish
    but have eternal life" (New International Version).

2   Surah 4.171 of the Qur'an, for instance, states, "People of
    the Book! Do not exceed the limits in your religion, and
    attribute to Allah nothing except the truth. The Messiah,
    Jesus, son of Mary, was only a Messenger of Allah."

Chapter 14: Fate

1   Hippolytus, third century CE, quoted by A. A. Long and D. N. Sedley in *The Hellenistic Philosophers*, vol. 1 (Cambridge: Cambridge University Press, 1987), 572–73.

2   John Sellars, *Hellenistic Philosophy* (Oxford: Oxford University Press, 2018), "Chrysippus on Physical Determinism" in chapter 6.

Chapter 15: Stoic Physics and Logic

1   Julia Annas, "Ethics in Stoic Philosophy," *Phronesis* 52, no. 1 (2007): 58–87.

2   See A. A. Long, "Stoic Eudaimonism," in *Stoic Studies* (Oakland: University of California Press, 2001), 179–201; and A. A. Long, "The Stoic Concept of Evil," *Philosophical Quarterly* 18, no. 73 (October 1968): 329–43.

Chapter 16: Stoicism in Summary

1   Christopher Gill, "What Is Stoic Virtue?," *Modern Stoicism*, November 21, 2015, https://modernstoicism.com/what-is-stoic-virtue-by-chris-gill.

Glossary

1   Christopher Gill, "What Is Stoic Virtue?," *Modern Stoicism*, November 21, 2015, https://modernstoicism.com/what-is-stoic-virtue-by-chris-gill.

Recommended Reading

It is our hope that after reading *What Is Stoicism?* you are better equipped to sketch out your own path to eudaimonia. To aid you further, we would like to recommend some additional reading resources.

Our recommendations are broken into four categories: formative, practical, advanced, and classic. *Formative* means something like "foundational" or "historical." *Practical* means "everyday helpful Stoic advice for everyone." *Advanced* means "nuanced, in-depth, and/or specialized." *Classic* means "ancient texts."

Formative Reading

Scott Aikin and William O. Stephens, *Epictetus's Encheiridion: A New Translation and Guide to Stoic Ethics* (London: Bloomsbury Academic, 2023).

Brad Inwood, ed., *The Cambridge Companion to the Stoics* (Cambridge: Cambridge University Press, 2003).

John Sellars, *Hellenistic Philosophy* (Oxford: Oxford University Press, 2016).

John Sellars, *Stoicism (Ancient Philosophies)* (Oxfordshire: Routledge, 2006).

Practical Reading

David Fideler, *Breakfast with Seneca* (New York: W. W. Norton, 2021).

Donald Robertson, *How to Think Like a Roman Emperor* (New York: St. Martin's Press, 2019).

Kai Whiting and Leonidas Konstantakos, *Being Better: Stoicism for a World Worth Living In* (Novato, CA: New World Library, 2021).

Advanced Reading

Julia Annas, *Intelligent Virtue* (Oxford: Oxford University Press, 2011).

Aiste Celkyte, *The Stoic Theory of Beauty* (Edinburgh: Edinburgh University Press, 2020).

Christopher Gill, *Learning to Live Naturally* (Oxford: Oxford University Press, 2023).

Christopher Gill, *The Structured Self in Hellenistic and Roman Thought* (Oxford: Oxford University Press, 2006).

Margaret Graver, *Stoicism and Emotion* (Chicago: University of Chicago Press, 2007).

Pierre Hadot, *The Inner Citadel: The Meditations of Marcus Aurelius*, trans. Michael Chase (Cambridge, MA: Harvard University Press, 2001).

Christoph Jedan, *Stoic Virtues: Chrysippus and the Religious Character of Stoic Ethics* (London: Continuum, 2010).

Will Johncock, *Beyond the Individual: Stoic Philosophy on Community and Connection* (Eugene, OR: Pickwick Publications, 2023).

A. A. Long, ed., *Problems in Stoicism* (London: Continuum, 2000).

A. A. Long, *Stoic Studies*, Vol. 36 (Berkeley: University of California Press, 2001).

Malcolm Schofield, *The Stoic Idea of the City* (Chicago: University of Chicago Press, 1999).

Classic Reading

Epictetus, *Discourses.* The majority of *Discourses* quotes used in this book are from (or are adapted from) *Epictetus: Discourses, Fragments, Handbook*, trans. Robin Hard, ed. Chris Gill (Oxford: Oxford University Press, 2014).

Epictetus, *The Encheiridion.* The corresponding quotes used in this book are from (or are adapted from) Epictetus, *The Encheiridion*, trans. Robin Hard, ed. Chris Gill (Oxford: Oxford University Press, 2014).

Marcus Aurelius, *Meditations.* The corresponding quotes used in this book are from (or are adapted from) *Marcus Aurelius: Meditations, with Selected Correspondence*, trans. Robin Hard, ed. Chris Gill (Oxford: Oxford University Press, 2011).

Musonius Rufus, *Lectures and Fragments.* The corresponding quote used in this book is from Cynthia King, trans., *Musonius Rufus: Lectures and Sayings* (CreateSpace Independent Publishing Platform, 2011).

Seneca the Younger, *Moral Letters to Lucilius.* The corresponding quotes used in this book are from (or are adapted from) Margaret Graver and A. A. Long, ed. and trans., *Lucius Annaeus Seneca: Letters on Ethics* (Chicago: University of Chicago Press, 2015).

About the Authors

Tanner Campbell is an American philosopher of Stoicism living in Newcastle upon Tyne in the United Kingdom. He is the creator of the *Practical Stoicism* podcast and newsletter, founder of the Society of Stoics, and creator of the course "Understanding Stoicism."

TannerCampbell.net

Kai Whiting is a lecturer and researcher and the coauthor of *Being Better: Stoicism for a World Worth Living In*. He has discussed Stoicism in publications such as the *Financial Times*, *UnHerd*, and *Vice*. He lives in Newcastle upon Tyne, UK.

StoicKai.com

NEW WORLD LIBRARY is dedicated to publishing books and other media that inspire and challenge us to improve the quality of our lives and the world.

We are a socially and environmentally aware company. We recognize that we have an ethical responsibility to our readers, our authors, our staff members, and our planet.

We serve our readers by creating the finest publications possible on personal growth, creativity, spirituality, wellness, and other areas of emerging importance. We serve our authors by working with them to produce and promote quality books that reach a wide audience. We serve New World Library employees with generous benefits, significant profit sharing, and constant encouragement to pursue their most expansive dreams.

We print our books with soy-based ink on paper from sustainably managed forests. We power our Northern California office with solar energy, and we respectfully acknowledge that it is located on the ancestral lands of the Coast Miwok Indians. We also contribute to nonprofit organizations working to make the world a better place for us all.

Our products are available wherever books are sold.

customerservice@NewWorldLibrary.com
Phone: 415-884-2100 or 800-972-6657
Orders: Ext. 110
Fax: 415-884-2199
NewWorldLibrary.com

Scan below to access our newsletter
and learn more about our books and authors.